W.E.B. DU BOIS

BY HILARY LOCHTE

Gareth Stevens
PUBLISHING

Please visit our website, www.garethstevens.com. For a free color catalog of all our high-quality books, call toll free 1-800-542-2595 or fax 1-877-542-2596.

Library of Congress Cataloging-in-Publication Data

Lochte, Hilary.
  W. E. B. Du Bois / Hilary Lochte.
      pages cm. — (Heroes of Black history)
  Includes bibliographical references and index.
  ISBN 978-1-4824-2920-6 (pbk.)
  ISBN 978-1-4824-2921-3 (6 pack)
  ISBN 978-1-4824-2922-0 (library binding)
  1. Du Bois, W. E. B. (William Edward Burghardt), 1868-1963—Juvenile literature. 2. African Americans—Biography—Juvenile literature. 3. African American intellectuals—Biography—Juvenile literature. 4. African American civil rights workers—Biography—Juvenile literature. I. Title.
  E185.97.D73L55 2015
  323.092—dc23
  [B]
                                        2015012440

First Edition

Published in 2016 by
Gareth Stevens Publishing
  11 East 14th Street, Suite 349
New York, NY 10003

Designer: Katelyn E. Reynolds
Editor: Therese Shea

Photo credits: Cover, p. 1 (W. E. B. Du Bois), cover, pp. 1–32 (background image), pp. 5, 13, 19, 23, 25 Library of Congress; pp. 7, 21 Buyenlarge/Getty Images; p. 9 Education Images/UIG via Getty Images; pp. 11, 15 Santiago Casuriaga/Wikipedia.org; p. 17 Quadell/Wikipedia.org; p. 25 Hulton Archive/Getty Images; p. 28 MyLoupe/UIG via Getty Images.

Printed in the United States of America

CPSIA compliance information: Batch #CS15GS: For further information contact Gareth Stevens, New York, New York at 1-800-542-2595.

CONTENTS

Words in the glossary appear in **bold** type the first time they are used in the text.

NEW ENGLAND CHILDHOOD

William Edward Burghardt "W. E. B." Du Bois (doo-BOYZ) was born on February 23, 1868, in Great Barrington, Massachusetts. His life began just 3 years after the American Civil War and the end of slavery.

W. E. B. Du Bois was raised by his mother Mary Burghardt and her family. He had very little contact with his father, Alfred Du Bois. Although they didn't have much money, Du Bois had a happy childhood. He was an excellent student. In 1884, he became the first African American to graduate from Great Barrington High School. Sadly, his mother passed away soon after.

SHELTER IN A SMALL TOWN

Du Bois grew up in the small town of Great Barrington as one of its few black residents. His classmates and playmates were all white. During his childhood, he didn't experience much **discrimination**. The equal treatment he received as a child shaped his beliefs for the rest of his life.

Today, the town of Great Barrington celebrates its connection to the early life of W. E. B. Du Bois. This is the town as it appeared in the 1930s.

5

A JOURNEY SOUTH

Du Bois couldn't afford to pay for college and worked as a reporter in Great Barrington after high school. Fortunately, a group of townspeople collected money so that he could attend Fisk University, a college for African Americans in Nashville, Tennessee.

Excited by the opportunity, Du Bois saw moving south as a chance to experience black life in another part of the United States. His childhood had sheltered him from the kinds of racial discrimination most African Americans faced during **Reconstruction**. In 1885, a 17-year-old Du Bois arrived in Tennessee and began a new life.

SEGREGATION

Segregation, the forced separation of races, became legal in the United States after the *Plessy v. Ferguson* Supreme Court case of 1896. The ruling said it was legal to make black people use separate public buildings and services, such as buses, restrooms, restaurants, and schools, as long as they were "equal" to those available to whites. (They often weren't.)

6

Du Bois's years at Fisk University were his first time surrounded by almost all African Americans as well as his first experience with the segregated South.

7

LESSONS IN SCHOOL AND LIFE

Life in Tennessee presented Du Bois with startling contrasts. At Fisk, he met wealthy, educated African American men and women, an experience so different from his childhood. Du Bois and his classmates lived a protected life at the college, but—off school grounds—Du Bois saw firsthand the **racism** of the post–Civil War South.

During college, Du Bois spent his summers teaching in **rural** Tennessee. This opportunity brought him in contact with poor African Americans whose lives still resembled the painful struggle of slavery. His experiences teaching shaped his views on education for years to come.

IS HARD WORK ENOUGH?

Du Bois learned much about poverty while teaching children from sharecropping families in Tennessee. His students were enthusiastic about school, but couldn't attend regularly because their families needed them to work in the fields. Du Bois worried that conditions for his students were too hard to overcome, even with education.

Sharecroppers were farmers who raised crops for the owner of a piece of land. They were paid a portion of the money from the sale of the crops. Many African Americans remained in poverty after the Civil War because of the sharecropping system.

9

FROM STUDENT TO SCHOLAR

W. E. B. Du Bois graduated from Fisk University in 1888 and returned to Massachusetts to follow his dream of attending Harvard University. At Harvard, Du Bois studied philosophy, earning a bachelor's **degree** in 1890. In 1892, he added a master's degree in history to his list of accomplishments.

STILL A HARVARD MAN

At Harvard, Du Bois succeeded in his classes, but didn't always feel welcome socially. Since he loved singing, he tried to join the school's glee club, but wasn't accepted. Du Bois felt that his race and lack of money made him an outsider at Harvard, but he didn't let this discrimination stop him.

Still thirsty for knowledge, Du Bois traveled to Germany and studied at Friedrich Wilhelm University for 2 years before returning to Harvard. Du Bois achieved his greatest education goal in 1895 when he earned his **doctorate** in history. He became the first African American to earn this high degree from Harvard.

Du Bois formed friendships with more professors than classmates at Harvard. They encouraged him in his work and his goals.

EDUCATOR AND RESEARCHER

In 1894, Wilberforce University, a college for African Americans in Ohio, hired Du Bois as a professor while he was still finishing his doctorate. There, he taught Greek, Latin, and later German.

Two years later, Du Bois accepted a position at the University of Pennsylvania. The school hired him to study the lives of African Americans in the city of Philadelphia. Du Bois spoke to and **researched** thousands of blacks. His much admired work, titled *The Philadelphia Negro: A Social Study*, was published in 1899.

Du Bois's next teaching position was at Atlanta University in Georgia, beginning in 1897. He taught there until 1910.

WORKING AGAINST RACISM

Du Bois believed that his research in Philadelphia would help fight racism. He was convinced that most racism was the result of white Americans not knowing enough about African Americans and their lives. Du Bois hoped that his study and other writings would help build understanding between people.

Du Bois's time at Atlanta University was happy.
He made many friends. However, he rarely left the school grounds.
Segregation laws made life in Georgia very hard for African Americans.

13

FAMILY AND TRAGEDY

Although Du Bois seemed to work and study constantly, he did find time for a personal life. While teaching at Wilberforce University, he met and fell in love with a student named Nina Gomer. They married on May 12, 1896, in Cedar Rapids, Iowa.

In 1897, Du Bois and his wife had a son, whom they named Burghardt Gomer Du Bois. In 1899, young Burghardt became ill with diphtheria, a serious disease that attacks the heart and nervous system. Atlanta had few black doctors, and Du Bois struggled to find a white doctor who would treat an African American child. Two-year-old Burghardt died on May 24, 1899.

TRYING TO HEAL

Du Bois and Nina were heartbroken after the loss of Burghardt. "The child's death tore our lives in two," he later wrote. In October 1900, the couple had another child, a daughter named Nina Yolande Du Bois. The little girl helped heal some of their sadness, but Du Bois said his wife never really recovered.

W. E. B. and Nina Du Bois were married for 54 years, until Nina's death in 1950. The couple is pictured here with Burghardt.

15

A MAJOR WORK

While working at Atlanta University, Du Bois's fame as a scholar and intellectual grew. He used his standing to address major issues facing African Americans such as racism and poverty. Du Bois regularly conducted research, published writings, and gave speeches and presentations in the United States and internationally.

THE TALENTED TENTH

Leadership was one of Du Bois's favorite topics. In a 1903 essay, he used the phrase "The Talented Tenth" to describe his vision of African American leadership. Du Bois argued that a small group of educated African Americans, like himself, was needed to lead the black community out of poverty and segregation.

In 1903, Du Bois published one of his best-known works, a collection of essays titled *The Souls of Black Folk*. In this book, he examined the impact of racism in the United States and suggested ways to fight it. *The Souls of Black Folk* is one of the earliest **sociology** publications and is still widely read today.

THE

SOULS OF BLACK FOLK

ESSAYS AND SKETCHES

BY

W. E. BURGHARDT DU BOIS

SECOND EDITION

A.C. McCLURG

CHICAGO
A. C. McCLURG & CO.
1903

In *The Souls of Black Folk,* Du Bois wrote how strange it was as a black American to be "always looking at one's self through the eyes of others." How white Americans saw him might be completely different from how he saw himself.

A PUBLIC DISAGREEMENT

The Souls of Black Folk caused a major public disagreement between Du Bois and another famous African American educator, Booker T. Washington. Du Bois and Washington held different views on the role of education for African Americans.

Washington was an advocate, or supporter, of the kind of **industrial education** offered at the Tuskegee Institute in Alabama. He believed that career training, such as farming, carpentry, and cooking, would lead to financial stability for African Americans. Du Bois advocated for classical education, similar to his own, because he felt it would produce future leaders and intellectuals within the African American community.

CHILD OF SLAVERY

Unlike Du Bois, Booker T. Washington was born into slavery, only becoming free when he was 9 years old, after the American Civil War. He earned a degree from Hampton Normal and Agricultural Institute and became a popular public speaker. In 1881, Washington was hired to establish the Tuskegee Normal and Industrial Institute in Alabama.

18

Tuskegee began as a one-room school with a class of 30 students. Booker T. Washington was the first teacher. He made the school into a well-respected institute.

Du Bois and Washington competed for the support of wealthy white people to fund their work. Du Bois was discouraged that Washington's popularity meant schools like Atlanta University that didn't focus on industrial education received less money.

Du Bois was worried that many white donors only supported Washington because schools like Tuskegee would keep African Americans in humble jobs that limited their access to power. He thought that Washington's views encouraged African Americans to accept the roles set for them by segregation. Du Bois wanted blacks to rise above the boundaries of segregation and saw education as the solution.

DIFFERENT, BUT NOT OPPOSITE

In private, both men understood each other's beliefs. Du Bois knew that industrial training would benefit many African Americans, and Washington knew that a classical education was important to create future black leaders. Both men cared deeply about helping African Americans, but couldn't agree on **priorities** or approaches.

Female students sit on the steps of Atlanta University around 1900. They received the kind of classical education supported by W. E. B. Du Bois.

21

THE NIAGARA MOVEMENT

In an effort to challenge the views of Washington and his backers, Du Bois founded the Niagara Movement in 1905. Du Bois gathered a group of 29 African American leaders in Niagara Falls, Canada, to discuss ways to fight segregation. Du Bois and members of the Niagara Movement wrote a "Declaration of Principles," demanding freedom of speech, the right to an equal education, and the end of segregation laws, among other things.

Although the Niagara Movement had some success, growing to more than 150 members in 17 states, it struggled financially. It couldn't get enough support in the Washington-favoring press to spread its message. By 1909, the Niagara Movement was over.

CROSSING THE BORDER

Du Bois originally planned for the Niagara Movement's first meeting to take place in the United States, in Buffalo, New York. However, he found the segregated hotels in Buffalo unacceptable, so he moved his group north to Niagara Falls, Ontario. The Canadian town welcomed Du Bois and his important guests.

Booker T. Washington sent a "spy" to the first meeting of the Niagara Movement. However, the spy went to Buffalo and couldn't locate the group! Du Bois is in the middle row, second from the right.

23

THE NAACP

Although the Niagara Movement folded, public support of equal rights for African Americans was growing. In 1909, white and black **activists** formed the NAACP (National Association for the Advancement of Colored People), a group dedicated to fighting discrimination and gaining equal rights for African Americans.

TAKING A RISK TO MAKE A DIFFERENCE

When Du Bois left Atlanta University to work for the NAACP, he was taking a true leap of faith. He didn't know if the new organization would be able to pay him or if it would even survive. Despite these doubts, Du Bois made the move from teacher to activist.

Du Bois left his teaching job at Atlanta University to work in New York for the NAACP. He became the first editor of the organization's magazine *The Crisis* and helped the NAACP grow into a powerful force in the fight for civil rights. The NAACP continues its social justice work today, more than 100 years later.

Under Du Bois's direction, *The Crisis* reported on discrimination and violence against blacks across the nation. It was a big reason for the growth of the NAACP and is still published today.

25

FIGHTING FOR PEACE

Du Bois served as editor of *The Crisis* until 1934, stepping down when he was 66 years old. He returned to Atlanta University and taught for 10 more years.

At the end of World War II (1939–1945), Du Bois was horrified by the destruction of the cities of Hiroshima and Nagasaki in Japan. He became a vocal antiwar activist.

ENEMY OF THE STATE

Du Bois's beliefs caused legal troubles. The US government accused Du Bois's antinuclear weapon organization, the Peace Information Center, of being funded by the Soviet Union. Du Bois was arrested, but a judge dropped the charges because there was no proof against him. However, the charges still did much damage to his good name.

He opposed the **Cold War** and spoke out against the use of nuclear weapons, views that were generally unpopular in the United States. Du Bois was accused of being a traitor. Despite these attacks, Du Bois continued to fight for causes he believed in.

Of his court case, Du Bois said: "It is a sad commentary that we must enter a courtroom today to plead 'Not Guilty' to something that cannot be a crime—advocating peace and friendship between the American people and the peoples of the world."

27

THE JOURNEY ENDS

Over his long and productive life, Du Bois had become internationally respected and received invitations from all over the world. At the age of 90, he went on a speaking tour of Europe, the Soviet Union, and China.

In 1961, Du Bois moved to the African country of Ghana in order to create an encyclopedia of Africa, an ambitious project for a man of his advanced years. Sadly, not even the tireless Du Bois could work forever, and his health finally failed. W. E. B. Du Bois died in Ghana on August 27, 1963. He was 95 years old.

PASSING THE TORCH

Du Bois died 1 day before the March on Washington for Jobs and Freedom, an event made possible, in part, by Du Bois's years of tireless work. Moments after Du Bois's death was announced to the crowd, Dr. Martin Luther King Jr. delivered the famous "I Have a Dream" speech.

sculpture at Du Bois's home in Ghana
WILLIAM EDWARD
B. DU BOIS

THE LIFE OF W. E. B. DU BOIS

1868 William Edward Burghardt Du Bois is born February 23 in Great Barrington, Massachusetts.

1884 Du Bois becomes the first African American to graduate from Great Barrington High School.

1888 Du Bois graduates from Fisk University.

1894 Wilberforce University hires Du Bois as a professor.

1895 Du Bois earns a doctoral degree from Harvard.

1896 Du Bois marries Nina Gomer.

Burghardt Gomer Du Bois is born.

1897 Du Bois accepts a teaching position at Atlanta University.

Du Bois's research for the University of Pennsylvania is published.

1899 Burghardt Du Bois dies.

1900 Nina Yolande Du Bois is born.

1903 Du Bois publishes *The Souls of Black Folk*.

1905 Du Bois founds the Niagara Movement.

1910 Du Bois becomes the first editor of the NAACP's magazine *The Crisis*.

1934 Du Bois steps down from *The Crisis* and returns to Atlanta University.

1963 Du Bois dies in Ghana on August 27.

GLOSSARY

activist: one who acts strongly in support of or against an issue

Cold War: the nonviolent conflict between the United States and the Union of Soviet Socialist Republics (USSR) during the second half of the 20th century

degree: a title presented to students by a college, university, or professional school on completion of a program of study

discrimination: treating people unequally because of their race or beliefs

doctorate: the highest degree offered by a university. It requires many years of study.

industrial education: training in practical, job-based fields such as carpentry or sewing

priority: something that is more important than other things and that needs to be done or dealt with first

racism: the belief that people of different races have different qualities and abilities and that some are superior or inferior

Reconstruction: after the American Civil War, the reorganization and reestablishment of the states that had left the Union

research: to study to find something new

rural: of or relating to the country and the people who live there instead of the city

sociology: the study of the origin, development, and structure of societies and the behavior of individuals and groups

FOR MORE INFORMATION

BOOKS

Bolden, Tonya. *W. E. B. Du Bois: A Twentieth-Century Life*. New York, NY: Viking, 2008.

Whiting, Jim. *W. E. B. Du Bois: Civil Rights Activist, Author, Historian*. Broomall, PA: Mason Crest Publishers, 2010.

Wittrock, Jeni. *W. E. B. Du Bois*. North Mankato, MN: Capstone Press, 2015.

WEBSITES

Reconstruction and Black Education
www.pbslearningmedia.org/resource/osi04.soc.ush.civil.reconstruction/reconstruction-and-black-education/
This video explores the struggle for education for black Americans after the Civil War.

W. E. B. Du Bois
www.americaslibrary.gov/aa/dubois/aa_dubois_subj.html
Read about Du Bois's life and work on this Library of Congress website.

INDEX